She *Laughs*

A Devotional with Motivational Quotes and
Life Lessons for the Overcoming Woman

ASHLEY JOY

She Laughs Without Fear of the Future

Editing by ChristianEditingServices.com

Interior/Exterior Graphic Design by I Karolyne Roberts from IAMIMAGE.COM.

Table of Contents

TABLE OF CONTENTS   5

DEDICATION   7

POEM   11

BIBLICAL WOMANHOOD   13

A WOMAN AFTER GOD'S HEART   14
THE COST OF FOLLOWING THE KING   21

THE OVERCOMING WOMAN   24

FAITH OVER FEAR   25
THE BEAUTIFUL STRUGGLER   32

THE ROYAL DAUGHTER   44

THE LORD CORRECTS THE WOMAN HE LOVES   45
LIGHT OF THE WORLD   52

THE SISTERHOOD   58

DIVINE CONNECTIONS   59
RUNNING YOUR RACE   65

THE GLOBAL WOMAN   68

HEIRS OF THE LAND   69
GOING TO THE NATIONS   77

THE WOMAN WHO PRAYS   83

Table of Contents

THE POWER OF A PRAYING WOMAN   84
QUEEN   88
THE STILLNESS OF HIS PRESENCE   91

THE WOMAN WHO LOVES   94

FORGIVEN LOVE   95
STRENGTH TO LOVE   104

ACKNOWLEDGEMENTS   107

ABOUT THE AUTHOR   109

NOTES   112

Dedication

This devotional is dedicated to the woman who has been talked about, discounted, heartbroken, discouraged, and who has cried many nights.

To my nieces: Dejah, Jayde, Milan and Mackenzie; Kira, Najae, and Amari

To Mommy

This devotional is dedicated to the heart of the overcomer in each of you.

With love,

Ashley Joy

"Blessed is she who has believed that the Lord would fulfill His promises to her!"

(Luke 1:45)

My Dear Sister,

I assume the woman who has this devotional has experienced a lot of life and made it through the fire. I assume there have been heartbreaks, sicknesses, discouragements, setbacks, and losses in her life. There have been times she had to cry, moments she had to fight, and lonely nights she spent on her knees in prayer. This devotional is dedicated to the woman who has been talked about, discounted, lied about, and cheated on. It is written to the woman who gave her all and got nothing in return and to all those who petitioned God, begging Him to turn their situation around.

My sister, I wrote this devotional to encourage and celebrate the overcomer in you. I compiled prayers, life lessons, and quotes from my own collection and from inspiring women worldwide who have also overcome the odds like you and me.

I pray this devotional reminds you just how precious you truly are in the eyes of our King. I pray that when situations occur, you can dig deeper into this devotional and learn from the experiences of others. My hope for you is that you'll study the pages to learn the significance of having a courageous faith and what it means to be a royal daughter. I pray that you will know God is calling you to go to the nations and become an ambassador for Christ as a global woman. I pray that when times get tough, you will understand that having a great sisterhood makes life's experiences easier. When it seems like the weight of the world is on your shoulders, you can always count on the joy of the Lord as your strength as His power enables you to become a supernatural woman, not a superwoman. My hope is that you will discover the power in being a praying woman. Finally, no matter what life throws your way, I pray you will always have confidence to laugh without fear of the future.

From my heart to yours,

Ashley Joy

Poem

Women of God can never be like women of the world.

The world has enough women who are tough;

We need women who are tender.

There are enough women who are coarse;

We need women who are kind.

There are enough women who are rude;

We need women who are refined.

We have enough women of fame and fortune;

We need more women of faith.

We have enough greed;

We need more goodness.

We have enough vanity;

We need more virtue.

We have enough popularity;

We need more purity.

- Maragarent D. Nadauld

Biblical Womanhood

A Woman after God's Heart

What does it mean to be a woman after God's heart? Charles R. Swindoll explains it best in his book *Becoming a Man or a Woman after God's Own Heart*. He says, "It means your life is in harmony with the Lord. What is important to Him is important to you. What burdens Him burdens you. When He says, 'Go to the right,' you go to the right. When He says, 'Stop that in your life,' you stop it. When He says, 'This is wrong and I want you to change,' you come to terms with it because you have a heart for God."

Wow! Being a woman after His heart can be very daunting. It can be hard to remove ourselves from the hustle and bustle of everyday life to hear God's voice for daily instruction. Trying to live biblically is hard work and sticking with it takes real commitment. So how do we become a woman after the Lord's heart? How do we focus all of our attention on eternal things instead of temporary things?

We must first understand that there are many options in life, but our best option as women is choosing the path that leads to eternal life. The Bible tells us this in Joshua 24:15: "But if serving the Lord seems undesirable to you, then choose for yourselves this day whom you will serve." God is looking for women who are completely His.

14

These women, like our biblical hero Mary, will gladly accept the calling on their life. They will confidently say, "I am the Lord's servant. May your word to me be fulfilled" (Luke 1:38).

A woman after God's heart isn't chasing the things of this world. Her desire is not for material possessions. Her heart discerns the differences between good and evil. She hears the sweet voice of her Shepherd directing her down the right path. Let us all become women after God's heart.

Prayer

Dear Heavenly Father, I desire to be a woman after Your heart. Give me the strength and ability to focus on Your love for me. Show me areas in my life that are not as You desire, and align my life with Your Word.

Meditation Scripture

"But if from there you seek the Lord your God, you will find him if you seek him with all your heart and with all your soul" (Deuteronomy 4:29).

❝A Christian woman does not put her hope in her husband, or in getting a husband. She does not put her hope in her looks. She puts her hope in the promises of God. She is described in Proverbs 31:25 [in the ESV]: 'Strength and dignity are her clothing, and she laughs at the time to come.' She laughs at everything the future will bring and might bring, because she hopes in God. She looks away from the troubles and miseries and obstacles of life that seem to make the future bleak, and she focuses her attention on the sovereign power and love of God who rules in heaven and does on earth whatever He pleases. She knows her Bible, and she knows her theology of the sovereignty of God, and she knows His promise that he will be with her, help her, and strengthen her no matter what. This is the deep, unshakable root of Christian womanhood. ❞

—Author/Preacher/Speaker John Piper from
www.DesiringGod.org

Dear Sister,

Let's talk about love. Let's talk about its ability to heal, transform, redeem, and restore us. I once knew of a thing called love. It was the topic of many discussions and almost every R&B and Pop song. I knew it was supposed to give me chills and satisfy my every desire. Love was designed to make me happy. I liked this love ideology; it was all about me and I was in hot pursuit of it. Anything or anyone that no longer satisfied me or made me happy was cut off, never to be spoken to again. No one was exempt. I called it "loving me." In time, I realized this love stuff hurts. After all, I wasn't experiencing the euphoric ecstasy that I had set my hopes on. I was confused and lost—so confused that I often mistook flattery for love, sex for intimacy, and truth for hate.

This destructive cycle continued until I was introduced to real love. Imagine a love so real that one would lay down His life and pay a debt He did not owe. Imagine a God so great with a love so intense that He would send His Son to serve as a substitute to suffer and die for our sins. In His time on earth, this Son would eat with sinners, heal the sick, restore sight to the blind, minister to the adulterous, wash the feet of those who would betray and deny Him, intercede for His accusers, suffer and die—all in the name of love.

Sister, this revelation, this gospel, changed my life. Love moved from being a flawed and self-serving ideology to the most real, the most beautiful truth I had ever known. It became the blueprint of how I viewed God, myself, and others. I frequently prayed, "Father, help me see others as you see them." He answered my prayer. He doesn't see people as pawns or commodities to be leveraged and traded. He sees them as full of purpose, beautiful, and valued. Most importantly, He sees them as debt-free. This perspective shook me to the core.

So now when someone sins against me, cutting them off isn't an option because I wasn't cut off. Why would I impose a debt that I didn't have to pay? Sister, with this new revelation of love, I moved from being a debt collector to an intercessor. I no longer looked to the world to define a love that I experienced every day. I no longer had to sacrifice my body on the altar of lust to draw close to a man, not when the God of the universe draws close to me when I draw close to Him. It's amazing! I promise I'll never forget it. I'll never forget the season when the gospel taught me how to love properly.

Humbly,

Nina Jackson
ProperGirl Inc.
www.propergirl.com

" Only when self moves out of the way can His spectacular glory come cascading through your life. When Jesus is in His rightful place, all insecurity will fade away and His lasting loveliness will become the mark of your life. **"**

—Leslie Ludy, from The Lost Art of True Beauty: The Set-Apart Girl's Guide to Feminine Grace

The Cost of Following the King

Following Jesus will cost you something. It may cost you your powerful position. It may cost you the respect of co-workers. It may cost you some friendships. It may cost you your livelihood. It may even cost you relationships with family members. There will be a cost. Abraham left his comfort, family, and home to travel to a foreign land. He stepped out in faith and the Lord directed him every step of the way. He was available to be used by God. How has Jesus "interfered with" your life? It's not about being comfortable as much as it is about being radical. Following the voice of God and moving when He says move may not always mean living a comfortable life.

Kyle Idlemon, author of the bestselling book Not a Fan, stated, "Most of us don't mind making some minor changes in our lives, but Jesus wants to turn our lives upside down."

Simply put, Jesus wants to do something radical in your life that you may not expect. This Christian life is going to shake you up and take you out of your comfort zone. We live to serve His purpose and see problems, possibilities, difficulties, and destiny as He sees them. If you want your relationship with God to be based only on your terms and your way, I ask you to reevaluate your relationship with our

King. Are you a fan or a follower? God is looking for people who are available to move when He says move. He wants to lead those who will trust Him beside the still waters, through the valley of darkness, and over the mountains into His marvelous light. What about you? Are you willing to take up your cross and follow Jesus wherever He leads? Are you willing to lay aside the things that make life comfortable and be captivated by the things of heaven? Are you willing to live a set-apart life even if others label you as extreme?

Prayer

Dear Heavenly Father, I am ready to be used for Your glory. I want to radically follow You and abandon my own will. Lord, allow me not to get comfortable with the temporary treasures of this world but aim for something even higher than myself.

Meditation Scripture

"Then he said to the crowd, 'If any of you wants to be my follower, you must turn from your selfish ways, take up your cross daily, and follow me'" (Luke 9:23 NLT).

The Overcoming Woman

Faith Over Fear

Let's face it: Most people live a fear-driven life. They live below their potential because they fear failure. Sister, I am here to tell you that fear will paralyze you—whether it is fear of heights, animals, sickness, death, or something else. Fear keeps people from living up to their full potential. It amazes me when I see how fearless children are. They dare to do things most adults will never do. However, we all were children at one point in life. So when did we adopt fear?

The very thing you fear the most is the thing you must face. I'm going to let you in on a little secret. For a long time I feared flying. I know you are thinking that's ludicrous since I'm an author who has traveled the world. Even so, days before flying I would get extreme anxiety to the point of sickness. When I got into the air, it did not get any better. Every bump, unusual noise, and the sound of wind blowing past the plane frightened me. I realized I didn't want to live that way anymore, and 65 percent of my life's work required me to travel. Can you imagine? I had no choice but to face my fear and continue to do so. I can't say I trust God and live in fear. I can't pray and worry.

Fear will cancel out faith. They cannot coexist. I was ashamed to be this way. It did not feel good to always be in a state of worry, anxiety, and fear. I had to look my fear in the eye and repeatedly recommit myself to faith in Christ. I challenge you to do the same thing today. Question your fear, challenge your fear, but most importantly, give your fear to God and allow Him to give you peace.

Prayer

Dear Heavenly Father, take out of me any and all fear that may be prohibiting me from living a full life in You. I want to live to my full potential and not be burdened by fear any longer. I trust You with my whole heart and no longer have to fear what may happen around me, to me, or in my future. My soul will forever be indebted to You. Amen.

Meditation Scripture

"So do not fear, for I am with you; do not be dismayed, for I am your God. I will strengthen you and help you; I will uphold you with my righteous right hand" (Isaiah 41:10).

66 There is in every true woman's heart a spark of heavenly fire, which lies dormant in the broad daylight of prosperity, but which kindles up and beams and blazes in the dark hour of adversity. 99

—American Author/Historian
Washington Irving

Dear Sister,

At the age of eleven, I believed the biggest lie this world could ever imagine. I believed that somehow I was a mistake and I was not supposed to be alive. The pain in my heart overwhelmed me as the memories of childhood molestation, bullying at school, and low self-esteem overwhelmed me. My frail spirit was not equipped to handle this type of emotional pressure. I took a shower and put on my best casual outfit. I sat on my bedroom floor and wrote a goodbye letter to my family. I went into the bathroom, poured ammonia from under the sink into a red cup, then sat down in front of the mirror in my bedroom. The side of the bottle said "deadly if consumed," so I figured this was the way to do it. I had decided I didn't want to live any longer. The pain of going on was too great in my eyes, so I put the cup up to my mouth and inhaled. The fumes from the cup made me dizzy and I dropped the cup. I started to cry. I knew in my heart I didn't want to die, but I could not take the pain of living. As I lay there on the floor—hurt, confused, and unsure of what to do—my mind was lost in thoughts and I was afraid of the future. I remember falling asleep in my tears.

While my mom and I were shopping a few months later, an older white woman invited us to church. She said, "Go to this church and praise God with all your heart, mind, and soul." My mom and I went the next Sunday. My mother gave her life to Christ. It took me a little longer, but eventually I did too. We never met that old white woman again. The church was all black so we would have seen her if she went there. To this day, we have never seen her again. We believe she was an angel sent by God to lead us to that church to get saved.

One Sunday evening while in the service, God filled me with His Spirit. No one laid hands on me. I remember feeling a presence overwhelm me and tears began to run down my face. I knew it was God. For the first time in a long time, I wanted to live. His love changed my heart, gave me strength, and commanded me to live again. I don't know why He did it, but I tell you, if He can redeem me from the pit of suicide, He can redeem you. No matter where you are and what you are doing, His love is able to cover you and pull you out of whatever condition your life is in. Think about the times you just couldn't understand but knew God had intervened. He is watching over you, Sister. He thinks of you all the time and He wants the best for your life. If He did it before, He will it do again. Let Him in.

"I am leaving you with a gift—peace of mind and heart. And the peace I give is a gift the world cannot give. So don't be troubled or afraid" (John 14:27 NLT).

Bridgette Reed
www.bridgettereed.com

"If through a broken heart God can bring His purposes to pass in the world, then thank Him for breaking your heart. "

–Evangelist and Teacher Oswald Chambers

The Beautiful Struggler

The Christian life is a constant struggle. If anyone told you that, in Christ, there wouldn't be any pain, suffering, heartache, loss, death, or sickness, you were sadly misinformed.

The apostle Paul reminded the Corinthian church that, although they may experience weakness and struggles, they must not lose heart—and neither should we. He also stated in 2 Corinthians 4:8 that we will become hard pressed on every side but not crushed, perplexed but not in despair, persecuted but not abandoned, struck down but not destroyed. Paul, a Christian, experienced numerous struggles that would have given anyone reason to lose hope. He was jailed, beaten, persecuted, and left for dead. He went without sleep and knew hunger and thirst. Paul understood his momentary troubles did not compare in any way with the eternal glory that would be his. Therefore, he lived by faith and not by sight. How can we adopt Paul's attitude when we face persecution, trauma, or any other earthly sufferings?

Sister, we must count our burdens and struggle as joy. God has fashioned us for this very purpose and guarantees us that what is to come is greater than what is now. We should never think we can achieve perfection in this earthly realm. Nonetheless, we are daily being perfected for His glory. Every season of suffering we experience makes us wiser, deeper, stronger, and better. This race is not for the swift but for the one who endures until the end. Don't lose hope. Continue to hold fast.

Prayer

Dear Heavenly Father, teach me how to handle life's struggles with joy. Teach me how to receive heartache and pain as a blessing. No matter what comes my way, show me that, in Your presence, I will find everlasting peace. Amen.

Meditation Scripture

"Therefore we do not lose heart. Though outwardly we are wasting away, yet inwardly we are being renewed day by day. For our light and momentary troubles are achieving for us an eternal glory that far outweighs them all" (2 Corinthians 4:16-17).

"For you have delivered
me from death and my
feet from stumbling, that
I may walk before God
in the light of life."

(Psalm 56:13)

Dear Sister,

Where do I start?
Life can be tricky,

But it can be liberating at the same time.

What usually prohibits us from reaching our true potential is fear of the unknown
Due to past failures that left scarred tissue,

Past rejections that hit a nerve so close to the bone that we barely speak of their existence,
Yet we allow the fear to linger.

I know
Because I've walked with them,
They have attached themselves to me,
Imposing themselves,
Controlling the channel of my thoughts,
Taking up residence,

Slowly becoming part of my psyche.

I stopped evolving and those thoughts began to evolve in me,
Making me comfortable accepting my misery and the notion of average living,
Conforming to my surroundings,

Just existing,

Which has been woven into the fabric of this country and woven

into the false identity of our people.

Yes me,

Accepting and not facing what I thought was my truth,

My obscured truth was that of belittling my intelligence,

Playing the background of someone else's frame of thoughts,

Having too many children running around playing this God awful

game of molesting,

Thinking that it was quite okay to let someone else touch me,

Yet not okay because, as I grew older, I couldn't really let a man get

close to me.

The spoken yet unspoken tragedy amongst me and my cousins fell

into a deadly silence of never communicating about our past

because "it's family,"

Amnesia overtook our thoughts, but it never healed our hearts,

It never eased the pain,

It jumped from relationship to relationship,

Even when we thought we had won the game,

Not the game of remembering but the game of forgetting,

Only to realize that it was only suppressed,

Suppressed thoughts that emerge and show their ugly heads when

least expected,

The Overcoming Woman

We became used to wearing the mask of dysfunctional love,

Until dysfunction reared its head at family gatherings and led to

fights and cursing one another out that sometimes did,

And sometimes didn't,

End with a drink or a hug.

Over time I began to realize that this was not normal,

Questioning a mom in spirit form at the age of eight as to why she

would leave me to bear this physical and emotional unrest,

Not sure of who I was back then,

But somehow I mustered up the urge to seek more,

For some strange reason,

My heart was not filled with hate but love that allowed me to

endure.

Our God sees all things and He was the light to my flame,

The glow in my shame,

He walked beside me in my darkest hour and kept me

So that I could share my story with my sisters of how I am a survivor.

Truth is

There is the public you,

The private you,

The spiritual you,

And the internal you.

The public you yearns for acceptance,

Yet the private you is all about perspective,

The spiritual you is searching,

And the internal you will emerge forever,

Know that the public and private you carry no weight with God,

But the spiritual and internal you are where He is waiting for you to

show up,

Take care of that and everything else will manifest.

The trick is not to get caught up and cloud your mind with racism,

classism, and past isms that never served you,

They were never for you to serve,

We are so caught up that we somehow pass these distractions

down from generation to generation,

Affecting our children,

Blocking their minds from the real meaning of freedom.

Freedom is knowing who you are in Christ,

Not forgetting your history or your ancestral story,

But being able to overcome it,

The Overcoming Woman

Allowing yourself to tap into your inner truth.

No longer do I let distraction captivate me,
It's designed of captivity and began to falsely tame us as people,

Taking residence in our mind unconsciously and consciously,

Keeping us blind until it became us,
So much so that we forgot about becoming.

Overworked,
Underserved,
Trapped in the matrix of wanting more but thinking that the life that
is happening right now is what we deserve,
Because that's all we ever heard,
Stagnant reality suffocating our dreams,

Trying its hardest to ruin them by toxic negativity that happens to
occupy the same oxygen space that we breathe,
How dare you want more than the life you were given
Is what is subliminally said,
But how dare you want less than what our Supreme Father has
divinely shared with you?

Open your ears and follow what He placed on your heart to do,
Create the world of your dreams,
It's fueled with purpose so His glory may be seen,

The created

Creating,

The masterpiece

Mastering the pieces,

Recognizing humanity,

Not knowing the how but trusting and displaying through your actions that no matter what your physical eyes may see, you still push forth because you ultimately believe,

You get to a point where you wake up knowing who you are in Him,

You see yourself becoming a true seeker and believer with unwavering faith even when you feel that all hope is lost,

Know that this is your time to be stronger and not to have faith with stipulations,

Don't get so caught up pondering your purpose that you totally miss the value,

Your value,

Your value comes from within,

Knowing that, with Jesus, you always have a friend.

Overcoming fear, disappointment, and rejection lets the air in,

The air of opportunity,

The glow of freedom,

The unraveling of blessings,

The knowing that you were never meant to fit in,

The uniquely, wonderfully made you began to really live as if you
were born again,
As the saying goes, "Many are called, but few are chosen,"

Be proud to be cut from a different cloth,
No one said the road would be easy, but it is rewarding.

I really can't tell you how my story ends because I'm still traveling the
road of the unknown,
But what I can tell you is that I'm not alone,
My faith in God withstands its own,
My past contains markers to help others and to prepare me for
where I'm going,
I'm okay with that because, on this side of things, I'm more
comfortable in my skin,
I see my beauty unfolding,
Knowing that it is not me but the God within me who is priceless and
worth knowing.

I share this with you, Sis, so you know you are not alone,
We are forever evolving,

So stand up,

Take back what's yours because,

As the heir of the Almighty King,

You have the right to Stiletto Rock your throne.

-J. Scott

Jae Scott

Image Consultant

www.jaescott.com

The Royal Daughter

The Lord Corrects the Woman He Loves

If you are like me, at times you struggle with receiving loving correction and discipline. Something about being corrected makes you feel like a failure, especially when the person you love and adore the most is doing the correcting. However, we must understand, as royal daughters, God's discipline proves His love. He understands the Christian life involves extreme focus, renewing of our mind, and daily surrender. We are not exempt from sin. Honestly, I think we have more temptations as Christian women because of our awareness of sin. Therefore, when God corrects us because we've fallen into worldly traps designed to destroy us, we must welcome His chastisement as a sign of love.

It personally took me a long time to realize God's correction was His protection. It is an opportunity for us to grow in His love and likeness. We must understand the God we serve is for us and not against us and His only desire for us is to live in the fullness of His love and peace. We can then gladly accept the discipline as a sign of His unfailing love and an opportunity to reignite our zeal for Him.

Sisters, we must understand that God will not ignore, excuse, or tolerate sin as though it does not matter. Sin separates us from Him.

He is holy, and because of His holiness, we, as His daughters, are subject to the same standard. The next time you are challenged with the issue of sin, I would like you to think of God's correction as a sign of His acceptance and recognition of you as His holy child. For the Word says, "because the Lord disciplines those he loves, as a father the son he delights in" (Proverbs 3:12).

How amazing is that? God delights in those He corrects. I do not know about you, but I gladly accept the correction of our Father if it's a sign of His love and acceptance of me into the royal family.

Prayer

Dear Heavenly Father, we ask that You continue to break our hearts for the things that break Yours. Continue to pierce our hearts when we do things that are displeasing in Your sight. Make us better. Make us a beautiful reflection of Your glory. Amen.

Meditation Scripture

"My son, do not make light of the Lord's discipline, and do not lose heart when he rebukes you, because the Lord disciplines the one he loves, and he chastens everyone he accepts as his son" (Hebrews 12:5-6).

66 Our deepest fear is not that we are inadequate; our deepest fear is that we are powerful beyond measure. It is our light, not our darkness, that most frightens us. We ask ourselves, who am I to be brilliant, gorgeous, talented, and fabulous? Actually, who are you not to be? You are a child of God. Your playing small doesn't serve the world. There is nothing enlightened about shrinking so that other people won't feel insecure around you. We were born to make manifest the glory of God that is within us. It's not just in some of us; it's in everyone. And as we let our own light shine, we unconsciously give other people permission to do the same. As we are liberated from our own fear, our presence automatically liberates others. 🌙🌙

—Marianne Williamson, from Return to Love

48

Dear Sister,

I used to live my life not really understanding what the Word of God meant by "your bodies are temples of the Holy Spirit" (1 Corinthians 6:19). For some reason, not having sex before marriage was the only way I was obeying this scripture. This became a strong conviction that no one could take away from me, which was good. I often found myself in situations where I was really tempted and would wonder, "God, how far can I go until it is considered breaking the rule?" But the fact is it has never been, is not now, and will never be about just obeying "the rule." In fact, it is about loving God so much that we will refuse to do anything that will hurt or disappoint Him.

Sexual intercourse was a no-no for me. Meanwhile, I did so many other things that dishonored my Creator. I allowed myself to get drunk at wild parties. I cursed. I allowed anger, bitterness, jealousy, envy, lustful thinking and desires, selfishness, fear, lies, insecurity, and low self-esteem to pollute my heart. I was walking away from God, but He still pursued me and rescued me from myself. That's how awesome He is.

Today I am a totally different person, and the Lord has opened my mind to that scripture. Everything that touches us touches God. We were created because He chose to create us, and we live because He wants us to live. He has chosen to make our bodies His dwelling place. Therefore, our body's ultimate and main purpose is to bring Him glory.

Dear sister, do not waste more time living for the world and its passions. Rather, spend time living for the only one worth living for, the King of kings. Align your dreams, your desires, your vision, and your thinking with His. Let the way you live, speak, walk, dream, think, move, breathe, dance, and love bring glory to Him.

I pray you will understand and realize how precious and valuable you are. I pray you will walk in the Spirit, speak in the Spirit, think in the Spirit, and live in the Spirit. Let all you are—body, mind, and soul—be the temple of the Lord, His house of worship, the dwelling place of the Holy Spirit. You will never come last by putting God first.

Live to honor Him and do your best, whatever it takes to have Him say, "Dear daughter, I am proud of you."

Love,

Doña Moleka
www.chosen-i-am.blogspot.com

"It is a tremendous freedom to get rid of self-consideration and learn to care about only one thing—the relationship between Christ and ourselves."

—Evangelist and Teacher Oswald Chambers

Light of the World

As royal daughters we are the salt of the earth, the light that dissipates darkness. The Bible says we are like a city on the hilltop that cannot be hidden. As daughters of light we understand darkness is everywhere. However, we let the light shine within us by distinguishing ourselves by walking, talking, loving, and forgiving differently, following the example of our Savior, Jesus. We diminish our light by being quiet when we should speak, by going along with the crowd when we should be set apart, by allowing sin to dim our light when we should be a beacon of truth. Most importantly, we diminish our light by not explaining or inviting others to share the light with us. As royal daughters it is the light of God that gives us the force to conquer darkness.

We must not be afraid to let our light shine so others can be drawn to Christ in us. God's glory is upon us and it breaks the darkest night that surrounds us.

Have you ever walked into a room and instantly felt that some of the people didn't like you even though they didn't know you? I have and it took me a long time to realize it was my light that diminished the darkness that was in that place. It was the light that broke the barriers of oppression, the yoke of the enemy, and the weariness of the atmosphere. God delights in using us to bring restoration, peace, forgiveness, and love into the various atmospheres we walk into daily. Because we are free from enslavement, we are saved from death by sin. God freed us for the purpose of sharing the light that is within us. How are you walking as a daughter of light?

Prayer

Dear Heavenly Father, thank You for bringing me into Your kingdom as Your royal daughter. I thank You for shining Your light through me so others may taste and see that You are good. Order my steps, dear Lord, so my walk can be pleasing to You. In Jesus' name. Amen.

Meditation Scripture

Who knows but that you have come to your royal position for such a time as this?" (Esther 4:14)

"God, make me so un-
comfortable that I will
do the very thing I fear."

—American Actress and
Storyteller Ruby Dee

Dear Sister,

I found my worth in work. Schoolwork, church work, housework . . . work, work, work . . . it was how I knew I had purpose. I came to this realization recently and quite abruptly. Had someone told me this about myself a year ago or even a few months ago, I'd smile and brush the comment off as misguided. "Surely, I find my worth in God," I'd reassure myself.

As a Type A personality, I always have to be doing something and I need to be doing it well. After all, the Word says, "Whatever you do, work at it with all your heart, as working for the Lord, not for human masters" (Colossians 3:23). Misusing that scripture, I'd stop reading—or at least paying attention—after "with all your heart." The scripture preceding that one speaks of not being a people-pleaser and doing things out of "the sincerity of heart." Was I doing this? It is very easy—and dangerous—to take the praises and rebukes of people and transfer them into how we presume God feels. God makes it clear that His ways are not our ways and His thoughts are not our thoughts. We must be careful that we are truly pursuing Him and not the approval of men and women. While your purpose may manifest itself in a form of work, be intentional to realize that work, in and of itself, is not your purpose. Affecting people, touching lives, changing communities, building the kingdom . . . these are your purposes. Walk in them boldly.

Even if you know you are valuable, I can guarantee that you have undervalued yourself in comparison to how God sees you. Your worth comes from God and God alone. That fact makes you the most valuable commodity on this planet. Pushing for good grades, the next promotion, the winning shot can all be great things, but they don't add to your value. Likewise, failures in these things don't take away from your value. You were bought at a high price long before you could do anything, say anything, or work anywhere.

"If you're a hard worker and do a good job, you deserve your pay; we don't call your wages a gift. But if you see that the job is too big for you, that it's something only God can do, and you trust him to do it—you could never do it for yourself no matter how hard and long you worked—well, that trusting-him-to-do-it is what gets you set right with God, by God. Sheer gift" (Romans 4:4-5 MSG).

Yours truly with much love,
JaNaé Bates, MTh
Fullbright Scholar
www.BlackGirlScotWorld.com

The Sisterhood

Divine Connections

There is something truly divine about cultivating a sisterhood. Mighty women must stick together and have one another's backs throughout the storms of life. As women we all can relate to being attacked, criticized, gossiped about, and betrayed by other women. We have compared ourselves with other women and one woman to another. We have been jealous and envious of others. Let's agree that women have been totally ungodly toward each other. And we all have been guilty of it. I cringe when I think about times I have been disorderly toward other women. As I've matured in my relationship with Christ, I have realized one of the most divine relationships we can have outside of the one with the Savior is with another woman. Sisterhood teaches us about ourselves. What a joy it is to have accountability, loyalty, and a bond with other women!

Throughout the Scriptures we have witnessed a beautiful display of sisterhood. We have read about the faithfulness and loyalty between Naomi and Ruth. However, the relationship I admire the most would have to be the sisterhood between Mary and Elizabeth. In what could have been the most daunting season of Mary's life, she found comfort in the presence of her female cousin and friend, Elizabeth. Not only did she face pregnancy as an unwed woman, considering the times, she may have also faced gossip, scrutiny, and feelings of doubt and uncertainty. But something precious happened when Mary visited her sister-friend Elizabeth. Upon embracing each other, they rejoiced in each other's presence. Elizabeth exclaimed to her, "Blessed are you among women, and blessed is the child you will bear!" (Luke 1:42).

Dear sister, as we navigate through life, let us connect and love on one another. Let us uplift and speak life into our sisters. Let us respect and continuously pray for the women God has placed in our lives.

Prayer

Dear Heavenly Father, teach me how to be loving and kind toward other women. Give me Your heart, Father, so I can see them as You do. Teach me to uplift, speak life, and encourage every woman I encounter. In Jesus' name. Amen.

Meditation Scripture

"Blessed are you among women, and blessed is the child you will bear!" (Luke 1:42).

“I'm trying to create a world where women get used to seeing other women celebrate women.”

—Author and Speaker
Ashley Joy

Dear Sister,

I know how it feels to think you are all alone on your Christian walk. You may feel all of the females your age are living for self and Satan. You may feel betrayed by people you once trusted and respected. You may feel too vulnerable to open up to new people. You take your cares to Jesus, but you are longing for sisters in Christ to relate to.

God desires for us to have godly friends to love, serve, and grow. Hebrews 10:24-25 tells us godly fellowship is needed to grow us and for us to exhort one another in Christ, love, good works, and other spiritual areas. Hebrews 13:16 tells us fellowship and good works are our reasonable sacrifice to God. He is always glorified through our godly connections. First John 1:3-4 tells us our fellowship with other believers adds joy to our life and by fellowshipping with other believers, we are also fellowshipping with God. You may fear getting hurt by other believers and non-believers, but 1 John 2:19 shows us God will expose the ungodly people who intend to hurt us and they will be separated from us. No believer is perfect; we all make mistakes and have hurt others, both intentionally and unintentionally. Allow God to restore your heart from the pain of past hurts, and forgive those who committed those hurts.

I received one of my biggest spiritual breakthroughs by fellowshipping with sisters in Christ, some of whom I had just met and others I had known for years without having heard their testimonies. During a young women's conference, these ladies shared very transparent testimonies through which God revealed to me that there is no mess too ugly to be turned into a beautiful message of God's love. My past was riddled with mess and sins I thought I needed to lock away because they were too ugly to testify about in church. And I hadn't told others about my deliverance from them. Through these women, God showed me there is nothing too ugly to be made beautiful by Him. Sister, I encourage you to pray to God for godly sisters to come into your life, and I encourage you to step out and be the friend to others that you would like to have. When you are a true friend and sister in Christ, God will allow sisters with pure motives to come into your life and bless you above and beyond all you expect and can imagine.

In godly love,
Corrie Gallien

"If there ever comes a time when the women of the world come together purely and simply for the benefit of mankind, it will be a force such as the world has never known."

—English Poet Matthew Arnold

Running Your Race

Sister, why are you comparing your life with another woman's? Do you know what you are saying to God when you envy, compete, and show jealousy toward another woman's portion? Just as you would not go into an art gallery critiquing an artist's work in front of her, why do you constantly critique yourself in the mirror in front of God?

It is so easy to get caught up in the social media frenzy and start looking at another woman's highlight reel (the good things they highlight through social media) and get discouraged about our lives. We think, "Wow, they have a perfect marriage, a lovely home, beautiful kids, great friends, and an amazing social life," but the truth of the matter is that no one's situation is perfect. You don't know their private struggles. You don't know what they went through in their marriage. You don't even know how many miscarriages they may have had.

We must stop envying and showing jealousy toward other women. Let us instead start celebrating and learn to stay focused on the road God has given us to walk. Even if you have to "unfollow" or "unfriend" people on your social media, do it. It's not healthy nor is it good for your self-worth if you're constantly comparing your situation to another's. Sister, you are unique and wonderfully made. If you only knew the freedom we have in Christ. He has called each and every one of us to experience this freedom. We are tailor made in the image of God and, as a member of the body of Christ, each of us represents a unique part of Him. There will never be another like you. He died for you so you could live.

There's nothing wrong with admiring another woman and looking at the steps she took to get where she is today. But there is everything wrong when you emulate her life and try to be her. Rest, Sister. Life is not a marathon. You do not have to compete with anyone. The only thing you should be comparing your life with is the Word of God and the woman you were yesterday.

Prayer

Dear Heavenly Father, teach me how to appreciate my portion. Give me the ability to run my own race and not be envious or jealous of anyone else's. Teach me to encourage and uplift other women and not compete or speak any negativity. In Jesus' name. Amen.

Meditation Scripture

"I have seen something else under the sun: The race is not to the swift or the battle to the strong, nor does food come to the wise or wealth to the brilliant or favor to the learned; but time and chance happen to them all" (Ecclesiastes 9:11).

The Global Woman

Heirs of the Land

Do you know we serve the King who has dominion over the whole earth? Everything belongs to God. Not only did He design the land of the living, but He also owns everything in it. And as daughters of the King, we have access to this land. What do I mean? I mean we can travel anywhere in the world with contentment, knowing Christ Jesus is the same God in Louisiana as He is in India. Our Father, our King, created the land and He reigns supreme. I want you to take a moment and truly wrap your head around that.

I have traveled around the world and I am confident, as David wrote in the Psalms, the Lord's goodness is in the land of the living. I have seen His hand on the lives of those who do not look like me or even worship as I do, but they are all God's children. I have seen places that do not look anything like where I grew up, but God created these places too. It's truly an awakening to the soul and makes you appreciate the artistic side of God. Surely He's the greatest artist ever, and as His daughters, we can appreciate the beauty of our Father's land.

In Genesis we read that God gave us dominion over the earth and as heirs, we have a responsibility to the land. We are not to abuse what God has given us and must encourage others not to as well. As His daughters, we can appreciate the beauty of our Father's land. The Bible says in 1 Timothy 4:4, "For everything God created is good, and nothing is to be rejected if it is received with thanksgiving." So the next time you go for a walk, do yourself a favor and have a "God view." Find the beauty around you and appreciate the environment. God gave us the earth and we are accountable to Him for how we use it.

Prayer

Dear Heavenly Father, I thank You for the beautiful land You have created. As an heir of this land, I understand I have dominion to go where You send me with the confidence that You dwell there. Give me a spirit of appreciation for the land of the living and everything that dwells in it.

Meditation Scripture

"See, the Lord your God has given you the land. Go up and take possession of it as the Lord, the God of your ancestors, told you. Do not be afraid; do not be discouraged" (Deuteronomy 1:21).

❝When it's all over, I want to say: all my life I was a bride married to amazement. I was the bridegroom, taking the world into my arms. When it is over, I don't want to wonder if I have made of my life something particular, and real. I don't want to find myself sighting and frightened, or full of argument. I don't want to end up simply having visited this world.❞

—Mary Oliver, from
When Death Comes

Dear Sister,

I used to be ashamed of God. I weighed other people's opinion of me as more important than what God thought of me. I was among the cabin crew for an airline in Dubai, and He told me to leave my job to go do a community outreach internship with a church in Cape Town, South Africa.

"But wait, God. It's not paid? How will I survive?"

"I am your provider," said the Lord.

Still, my bank account didn't look like I could just up and go to another continent for an entire year, so I stayed at my job one more year to save up.

That was a mistake. I was no longer graced to be where I was. I learned that when the Lord says go, you should go. There was a reason why He wanted me to go at the appointed time. That additional year was the worst year career-wise. Everything went wrong, but that was a good thing because it showed me God had my back and He knew what was best for me. My identity was in my job and what others thought of me. But, Sis, true success is obeying God and doing what He has called you to do.

At the time, I had also based my obedience on my bank account, but anyone can save up money and move to another country, right? How does God get the glory from that? There was a reason God wanted me to go with a certain amount of money so I could not boast in what I had done and how I was able to get myself there. I wanted the move to look as normal as possible. But I am happy that God weaned me from my selfishness and stripped away the pride that would have only harmed me in the long run. He turned around what was meant for my harm into something good.

"'As for you, you meant evil against me, but God meant it for good, to bring it about that many people should be kept alive, as they are today. So do not fear; I will provide for you and your little ones.' Thus he comforted them and spoke kindly to them" (Genesis 50:20-21 ESV).

In January 2013, I moved from Dubai to South Africa. Just like God promised, He has provided. Although I am not making money, I feel like I'm making a million dollars. Just like He sent me here, He has sent others to provide for me. I am content, fulfilled, and at peace. And there is nothing I did to feel this way but be exactly where God called me to be. He has huge plans for you, Sis, and my prayer is that you will listen to Him and not those who are telling you to do the opposite of what God is telling you to do. Remember, not everyone will understand what God has called you to do because He has put the vision in your heart, not theirs. Therefore, it is important to guard your heart and discern who you allow to talk to your heart. You have to protect the vision God has entrusted you with. I promise stepping out in faith and doing what God has called you to do will be the most fulfilling and rewarding thing you can do in your life. At that point you will be at your ultimate high. Now, instead of feeling ashamed, I feel awakened to my purpose. Instead of worrying about others' opinions, I don't care because I live for an audience of One. Continue to seek Jesus. Be a light and do not dim it for anyone. God is always faithful. He will never leave nor forsake you.

"Be strong and courageous. Do not be afraid or terrified because of them, for the Lord your God goes with you; he will never leave you nor forsake you" (Deuteronomy 31:6).

Love,

Juliette Bush

International Missionary

www.julietheexplorer.com

"No enthusiasm will ever stand the strain that Jesus Christ will put upon His worker, only one thing will, and that is personal relationship to Himself which has gone through the mill of His spring—cleaning until there is only one purpose left—I am here for God to send me where He will."

—Evangelist/Teacher/Author
Oswald Chambers

Going to the Nations

As daughters we have access to our Father's land, and we can go wherever He sends us for His glory. One of the greatest commands Jesus gave before He was taken from this earth was this: "Therefore go and make disciples of all nations" (Matthew 28:19). The words go and nations are the two words that stand out to me the most. What are we doing? Going into the nations. Why are we going? To make disciples by spreading the good news. That was His mandate before Christ left the earth. As I mentioned previously, Jesus is the Lord of the earth and His salvation is for all people. The gospel is not for only one part of the world, and as daughters of the King, we have to go and make sure people in unreachable places hear the good news. This mandate was not an option; it was a command. Like other commands in the Bible, we have to obey it. We have to walk confidently in our various gifts, talents, and purposes, knowing God placed them on the inside of us to reach those unreachable places. We can find comfort in knowing He is omnipresent, protecting, guiding, comforting, and gives us the words to say.

The uniqueness of our gifts represents the diversity of God. As His daughters we must be represented in every industry, state, government, and household around the world. We are not limited to the four walls of a church building. Our going must not be for our own self-promotion. Our going must not be motivated by self-glorification. Our going must solely be for the glory of God. We are to bring honor to His name in every nation by delivering, baptizing, preaching, and teaching for Christ's sake.

What is your motivation, Sister? Why do you desire success? Are you concerned about spreading the good news or promoting yourself? Are you a mirror reflecting God's glory?

Prayer

Dear Heavenly Father, teach me how to be bold for Your name. Allow me to be in the right place at the right time and in my godly mind. Equip me to share the good news in all corners of the earth. In Jesus' name. Amen.

Meditation Scripture

"Therefore go and make disciples of all nations, baptizing them in the name of the Father and of the Son and of the Holy Spirit" (Matthew 28:19).

“Patience is more than endurance. A saint's life is in the hands of God like a bow and arrow in the hands of an archer. God is aiming at something the saint cannot see, and He stretches and strains, and every now and again the saint says—'I cannot stand anymore.' God does not heed, He goes on stretching till His purpose is in sight, then He lets fly. Trust yourself in God's hands. Maintain your relationship to Jesus Christ by the patience of faith. 'Though He slay me, yet will I trust in Him.

—Evangelist/Teacher/Author
Oswald Chambers

Dear Sister,

When I graduated college, I had my entire life planned. I was going to get my Masters of Science in Computer Science from USC, and I was going to live in Los Angeles as a developer for the rest of my life. However, God had other plans. He stirred up my spirit and I realized I was not following His path. Being very stubborn, I continued on the way I wanted to take, but it was the worst thing I've ever done. I dreaded going to class, and I found no joy in life. However, I had a full fellowship to attend one of the best schools in America and I was living in one of the largest cities as well. I continued to ignore God's voice and I was determined to live out my dream.

Eventually I could not ignore Him any longer. I am very thankful I had a great church in Los Angeles, First A.M.E. I also had a great relationship with our young adult pastor. Through prayer and counseling, I gained the courage to change my path and follow God's. I moved back to Cleveland, Ohio, and enrolled at Cleveland State University to receive my Masters of Science in Industrial Engineering–Systems Management. I loved every class, even the difficult ones. Even when I received criticism for leaving Los Angeles and walking away from a full fellowship, I knew what my purpose was and I ignored the naysayers. Upon moving back to Cleveland, I was able to get involved with my community through various social organizations and help inner city youth. I have also been able to help young college students through my current job, which is exactly what I believe God has planned for my life.

Through these series of trials, God has taught me He is always in control. I had my life mapped out perfectly until God shook things up. Through these trials, I have learned to listen to my heart and to God. If you're not in the right situation, your spirit will be bothered constantly. You will feel like there is something out of place. Once I began to follow God's path, my spirit was calmed. Even through the trials I faced after moving back home, I was still at peace because I knew I was doing exactly what God had planned. Every day of my life isn't perfect and I still continue to face new trials constantly. However, I know these trials are only preparing me for what God has in store for me and I am exactly where He wants me to be.

Jennifer A. Hairston
Engineer

The Woman Who Prays

The Power of a Praying Woman

I am convinced that when a woman prays, the windows of heaven open and the Lord listens carefully. (I am not saying that men's prayers are not effective. There are many stories in the Bible about men praying.) What I am saying is women have a unique ability to speak our heart's desires with authority, sincerity, and urgency. Look at Hannah in 1 Samuel 1:10. She was probably at the lowest point in her life, desperate for the Lord to answer. "In her deep anguish Hannah prayed to the Lord, weeping bitterly." Hannah was praying in her heart. Like Hannah's son, I know my brother and I are products of a mother's prayers. Our mother interceded on our behalf.

Many other women who are mothers, wives, grandmothers, sisters, aunts, and mentors have diligently interceded for their loved ones. Perhaps you too have done the same. You have seen results from the time spent with our heavenly King, not only in their lives but in your own as well. What Hannah teaches us about prayer is that the Lord is always near and He hears the cries of the brokenhearted. Only God could have answered her prayers and given her what she wanted in her time of need. One thing you need to remember about being a woman of prayer is that no matter how you feel or how troubled you are, God always has the solution to all of life's problems. Going to your friends or mentor is okay, but going to God will give you revelation and the peace that surpasses all understanding.

I've learned that as women we have a unique gift from God called intuition. We are able to discern the needs of our families, friends, children, and so forth. We must willingly go to the King on their behalf, interceding and petitioning. That's why it's imperative that you continue to keep your spirit away from petty drama, confusion, and reckless living. You have a responsibility to be a woman of prayer. A woman full of God's power and spirit. A woman who operates in harmony with the Holy Spirit and obeys what He is constantly speaking. You must be a woman with a transformed heart who does not see things in the natural, instead sees everything in the Spirit. What does that look like? Do you set aside time each day to pray? How important has prayer become in your life?

Prayer

Dear Heavenly Father, as a woman of faith, I understand how important my prayer life is—not only to myself but my relationships as well. Lord, teach me how to pray. Teach me what to pray for and show me those for whom I should pray—even if they don't ask. Use me as a vessel to petition and intercede on behalf of others.

Meditation Scripture

"Look to the Lord and his strength; seek his face always" (1 Chronicles 16:11).

66 I pray because I can't help myself. I pray because I'm helpless. I pray because the need flows out of me all the time—waking and sleeping. It doesn't change God—it changes me. 🌙🌙

—Poet/Novelist/Literary Critic
C.S. Lewis

Queen

There are many roads in life,

Where will you go?

Many questions to life,

Some answers you'll never know,

You stand before others already a queen.

People don't only hear your words, but they listen to what they mean,

Everyone has a purpose,

They possess qualities that have yet to reach the surface,

Life is a lesson, so don't lose focus.

Love is a crazy thing, even more crazy when you're in it alone,

When you can't image life with it gone,

In the end it's a valuable lesson learned,

Love is something many boys have yet to understand,

But remember understanding increases as boys grow into men.

To cause hurt is not in God's plans,

You can't be hurt if you place your life in His hands,

Always remember to value your worth,

Love does not cause hurt,

Pain is inevitable, but suffering is optional.

You are so beautiful,

Time is of the essence and you are the essence of life,

So hold your head up and you will always be alright,

You are already a queen,

God has given you your crown.

In order for a young man to be your king,

He must first realize he's an angel without wings,

Until then you may be on your own with God by your side,

Continue to pray for others,

And always remind yourself you are already a queen.

−Dr. Shawana S Gray

"We only trust people we know. If you're struggling to trust God, it may be because you don't really know God."

—Evangelist/Preacher/Author Martha Tennison

The Stillness of His Presence

Have you ever been in a place in your spiritual walk where all you desired was to sit in the presence of God and try to soak up all He had to offer? Maybe you needed to be comforted. Maybe you needed answers. Whatever your reason, you knew only God could supply what was needed. If you haven't already, you definitely will come to that place, maybe more than once. What I learned about the character of God is this: He desires to share intimacy with us, not just occasionally but all the time. He desires for both you and me to come into His presence so He can pour His goodness into us. But the truth is it's not always that easy for us to come. The enemy doesn't like it when we spend time with our Father. He sends all type of distractions. We try to get ourselves together before we go into God's presence because we know that getting close to Jesus means we can no longer hide our inadequacies. Intimacy is threatening. His light exposes our darkness, which causes us to come face-to-face with our inner selves. Unconsciously, we flee from God's presence because, if we didn't, we would have to answer to a higher mandate. Intimacy with God will require us to leave our comfort zone, and let's be honest, we don't like being uncomfortable.

What I love about our heavenly Father is that despite our unfaithfulness, He's still faithful. He's a gentleman who pursues us and is patient with our timing. He waits for us to come running into His arms and when we get there, He doesn't ask, "What took you so long?" Instead, He shows us what has been available for us the entire time. That's such an ideal relationship, is it not? Don't we desire to be accepted and forgiven when we mess up? Don't we want to experience grace? Don't we want a love that will transform us into better women? I can honestly admit, sisters, I searched high and low to fill that longing, that void in my heart. I tried men, material possessions, and parties—even alcohol. However, it wasn't until I got into the presence of my King and experienced His great love that I became stronger, more confident, and was able to go forth in life with the joy I so desperately desired. Intimacy is sanctification. It's a relationship that doesn't need a third party. All God asks is that you show up, be willing to listen, act on what you hear, and respond accordingly to discipline. Are you willing to open your heart to receive all He has for you? Are you willing?

Prayer

Dear Heavenly Father, teach me to be still in Your presence. Cleanse my heart from anything that's prohibiting me from being quiet before You. Renew my heart so I can dwell in Your presence. I need more of You each day. In Jesus' name. Amen.

Meditation Scripture

"Love the Lord your God with all your heart and with all your soul and with all your strength" (Deuteronomy 6:5).

The Woman Who Loves

Forgiven Love

We have been influenced by our culture to believe that love is conditional, that it is based upon how other people behave toward us. Therefore, if a person is kind and loving toward us, then we reciprocate by being kind and loving toward them. However, this was not the case with our hero and Savior, Jesus Christ, who took the road less traveled. He responded differently. Jesus not only forgave all humanity, He also died for the very people who nailed Him to the cross. Can you imagine that? One of Jesus' last comments to His Father was this: "Father, forgive them, for they do not know what they are doing" (Luke 23:34). This is a phenomenal example to us of how we should handle unjust treatment. Jesus' words were not only thoughtful but also unimaginable for a man who endured the unbelievable agony and suffering He did. He demonstrated the greatest example of what it truly means to love and forgive others.

Remember, the responsibility for the outcome of your destiny is in your hands. Forgiveness is not about the people who hurt you. It is all about you and your response to that hurt. Do not allow what they did or did not do to hold you in bondage. And if you are waiting for them to apologize before you forgive them, then you have given those people more power over you than they should have. Only victims carry hatred in their heart and make "why me" speeches. You are a victor in Christ. You are more than a conqueror! It is only by God's grace and sacrificial love that we are able to offer grace to others with the same measure it has been given to us. Therefore, because God freely loves and forgives us, we should freely love and forgive others.

Prayer

Dear Heavenly Father, teach me how to humbly forgive those who have done me wrong as you have forgiven me. Lord, I release any unforgiveness that's in my heart. Give me a heart that's not easily offended so I can continue to bring glory to Your name.

Meditation Scripture

"Three things will last forever—faith, hope, and love—and the greatest of these is love" (1 Corinthians 13:13 NLT).

"Have enough courage to trust love one more time and always one more time. "

—Storyteller/Actress/Author Maya Angelou

Dear Sister,

All my life I had everything planned and figured out while still declaring, "I trust you, Lord. Have Your way." I didn't mean it though. How could I when the minute my life seemed as if it had fallen apart I cursed and questioned, "Why me?" Why not me? I had every stipulation in the world as to why I was not going to get married and why I did not want to have children. I simply didn't have time to be "like most women" as I categorized them (naïve I know). Naturally, a million things swarmed through my head and I was terrified of being divorced—before I even walked down the aisle. Life was the last thing I was speaking into this marriage. My husband and I married and everything seemed amazing. Then the enemy swooped right into our happiness. My husband fell short and he cheated. When a spouse cheats, it's not easy to forgive. Instead, it breaks down everything you ever thought you knew about them.

I mean, Sister, how could this be happening to me? God knew my list of qualifications included the fact that I would never tolerate cheating. "Once a cheater, always a cheater," as they say. Right? Wrong! "Therefore, if anyone is in Christ, the new creation has come: The old has gone, the new is here!" (2 Corinthians 5:17). Instead of mending things and getting to the root of the issues, I chose to portray happiness on the outside, but inside I was bitter, confused, hurt, and felt abandoned. My faith shouldn't have resided in my husband. It should have resided in God. I knew exactly who

He was and what He was capable of doing. I delved so deep into the Word that I realized we all make mistakes. Yes, the Bible speaks about divorce within the realms of infidelity, but it also speaks about grace, mercy, forgiveness, restoration, and destiny. I choose the latter. I chose to be wise in how I lifted up my husband and in how I went to God.

This life is not mine. I am a living example of Him. It took something so dramatic for me to realize that I do have to be willing to give myself away so He can use me. As for the life I had planned for myself, I have learned that goals are good but God is better. I encourage you, Sis, whatever the enemy throws your way, God can redeem to glorify His name. Anyone can be made anew. This process taught me that my husband actually wasn't the issue. I was! Crazy, right? While I was yelling and screaming that I would never do something like that to him, saying he was less of a man and asking what kind of a father he would be to our future children if he couldn't treat their mother right, I didn't realize I was tearing down the very thing we were trying to build: our faith and foundation. Sister, give yourself to our Father. He knows what good things He has in store for you.

Victoria
Educator
Email: Vj1833@gmail.com

"Love recognizes no barriers. It jumps hurdles, leaps fences, penetrates walls to arrive at its destination full of hope."

—Storyteller/Actress/Author
Maya Angelou

Dear Sister,

Imagine you are riding in the passenger seat of a luxury car, your husband in the driver's seat, and a state-of-the art navigation system in the dashboard. You are taking a road trip somewhere neither of you has ever been, so you decide you will bring a road map along just to be on the safe side. As your husband is listening to the navigation system, you are also checking the map, frequently giving him directions you think are helpful. But he can't hear the navigation system over your "helpful" directions, so you end up lost. This sounds silly, but I used to do it all the time. While my husband was trying to listen to God, I couldn't help but try to take over. I was more concerned than submissive.

God used this same illustration in my marriage to reflect the way I treated Him in our relationship. While God and my husband had already planned the best way to get me to my future, I had a backup plan because I didn't truly trust either of them. When God exposed my heart to me, I realized it was nothing they had done to lose my trust. I had never really given it to them. On the surface I looked healed, but in my heart I was still broken and unwilling to submit. The Lord revealed that without submitting to Him, I could never submit to my husband. He broke my will by showing me who I really was.

Instead of looking at submission as a burden, I can see it as a privilege. My strength is found in surrendering my will to God's and the plans He has for my marriage—with my husband taking the lead. I can trust both of them to make the right decision because they have my best interest at heart. Submission is not about being told what to do; it's about trusting that God has placed a capable man at the head of your household. Your faith and behavior should show the goodness of Jesus to your husband, and by submitting to the will of God, you will submit to your husband.

So just relax and enjoy the ride. They have everything under control.

Chante Truscott
Founder, Wives in Waiting
www.WivesAndWaiting.com

Strength to Love

It is only through Christ we will receive the strength we need, the strength that will empower us to love. It is what keeps us living and operating in the fullness of God's rich glory. We were built from love. It is easy to love those who love us, but you and I need to learn to love the unlovable, to be kind to the evil, and bless the wicked. Only love dissipates the darkness. It is the most powerful motivation in the world. Once you start to believe that you are no longer loved, cared for, and valued, your heart starts to harden toward God and others. Every human being needs to be loved. Not one of us can tolerate being hated and unloved. Love is what ignites us and it is beautiful, especially when its foundation is based on God's design. It gives you rest and allows your mind to be at peace. That is why whatever is prohibiting you from loving is robbery—whether it is bitterness, fear, or unforgiveness. You are disregarding the very foundation on which you were born.

God is the most powerful source of love, and if you do not come to know Him intimately, you will never be able to love properly. At times when I just sit and meditate on the love of Christ, it totally overwhelms me. It truly surpasses my understanding. I never thought I could love as widely, deeply, and purely as I do in Christ.

As if sending Jesus to die for me was not enough, the Father constantly reminds me of His love through people, places, and all sorts of circumstances.

God truly desires you, Sister. He longs for you to spend time alone in His presence. He wants to be your refuge in suffering. He offers you a joy that is greater than the "happiness" this world can offer. I have observed that the best comforters and encouragers are those who know something about personal suffering. They have seen God's power firsthand and they are able to securely love others through their own suffering. Is that what you truly desire? Do you want the Creator of love to introduce you to an eternity of love? Do you want to suffer for Christ and still find peace amidst it all? If so, let Him make His home in your heart as you trust in Him. It is all yours—available and paid for. By God's grace, you can find the strength in Christ to say yes to Him.

Prayer

Dear Heavenly Father, give me the strength to love others unconditionally. Give me Your heart, for mine can be deceitful. Grace me to be a woman who loves. One who, most importantly, shows others the love of Christ. In Jesus' name. Amen.

Meditation Scripture

"*Love each other in the same way I have loved you*" (John 15:12 NLT).

Acknowledgements

Acknowledgements

First giving honor to God and His precious son Christ Jesus whom I owe all that I am!

I would also like to thank my husband Michael, for his loving support and contribution to my life. Baby, you inspire me to strive for excellence daily. I love you!

Thank you to my parents, Jean-Michael and Jayne Argentin, my protective big brothers and my beautiful nieces and nephews.

To Christian Editing service for providing me with a beautiful manuscript that I feel confident to share with the world.

To Karolyne Roberts and IamImage team for their patience in helping me self-publish my second book. Thank you for your commitment to excellence and seeing one of Gods child manifest in destiny.

To the many overcoming women all over the world, I thank you for daring to be healed and whole. I pray you'll always see the light at the end of the tunnel.

About the Author

About the Author

A consultant and communications professional, Ashley acclaimed as a emerging leader by her peers and mentors, continues a legacy of being civically engaged, culturally connected and spiritually led. Dedicated to her life's mission, she aspires to teach and instill a sense of purpose in everyone she comes in contact with. Given many platforms throughout classrooms, communities, air-waves, programs and initiatives across the country, She brings a guiding light on pressing social issues. She has collaborated, volunteered and worked with many churches, schools, and corporations. She's also facilitated numerous workshops with youth including her most popular titled "Self Justice is Social Justice" and "Media Impact: The Influence on Urban Youth" and "So You Think You Have Vision, Now What?" Any aspect of personal development through education, and religion has been the driving force in all that she embarks upon.

Born in Bridgeport, Connecticut she grew up in New Orleans, La and claims the Bayou City as home. Ms. Ashley attended Wilberforce University in Wilberforce, Ohio and received her Bachelor of Science in Business Management. Thereafter, she continued her education and studied at the Academy of Art University in San Francisco, California and received her Masters of Art in Media Communications.

About the Author

Despite her various appointments, Ashley know that she "is" because so many people who has gone before her "were". She's a beneficiary of a family and community who has wrapped their arms around her, and demanded greatness. Also, physically, mentally, and spiritually supported her pursuits. She is currently living, working and traveling abroad across the European continent speaking on various topics of women empowerment.

Notes

Notes

Notes

Notes

Made in the USA
Monee, IL
13 January 2022

88834569R00066